DEADMAN'S

By Oakley Dean Baldwin

Copyright © 2015 ODB Publishing

Check out my other stories and books at:

http://thebaldwinstories.wix.com/author-blog

The following is a family story from my 3rd Great Grandmother Margaret (Yates) Hale written June 16, 1925 in Clintwood Virginia. A story about some of the events and predicaments that she found herself in surrounding the Civil War (1861-65) and growing up in the 19th Century in the Appalachian Mountains.

This work is based mostly on family history, historical facts, court documents, tombstones, and newspaper articles that were available at the time of writing; gathered from multiple sources and pieced together into a plausible story. As such, it should not be considered a definite source of information. I am listing this story as fiction based on a true family story.

This story covers the tragedy of the loss of life, home, and imprisonment of Margaret Hale's family.

TABLE OF CONTENTS

Prologue

My 3rd Great Grandmother, Margaret Yates was born October 3, 1835 in McClure Creek Virginia; this story is about Margaret and as you will see in Chapter Six she documents her memories including stories that her grandmother Nancy (Sutherland) Yates told her from the time she was a young girl and well into her years as a young woman.

Margaret's grandmother, Nancy (Sutherland) Yates was born during the Revolutionary War circa 1780 and died at the start of the Civil War in 1861.

It was a wonderful feeling to find a story from family members that lived during the Revolutionary and Civil War periods.

We are very fortunate that Margaret agreed to tell this story when she did, and someone recorded it, because Margaret passed away just weeks after giving this information in 1925.

Margaret's grandfather was John Yates. John was also born circa 1780 during the Revolutionary War in Bedford Virginia and died in 1826 in Kentucky.

John Yates parents were Lt. Colonel William Yates and Mary Jane Henry. Lt. Colonel Yates was a 1764 graduate of the College of William and Mary in Virginia.

John's mother, Mary Jane Henry, was the sister of Virginia's first and sixth Governor Patrick Henry.

Lt. Colonel William Yates is said to have served on General George Washington's staff and was a Colonel in the department of muster-master-general during the Revolutionary War.

Lt. Colonel William Yates parents were Colonel William Yates and Elizabeth Randolph. Colonel William Yates was the fifth president of William and Mary College.

Elizabeth Randolph's grandparents were Colonel William Randolph and Mary Isham. They were the progenitors to three Virginia Governors and one acting Governor namely, the seventh Governor of Virginia, Edmund Jennings Randolph, and the eighth Governor of Virginia Beverley Randolph.

Later down the time line of History, Payton Randolph was the acting Governor of Virginia between the seventeenth and the eighteenth Governors. And the twenty first Governor of Virginia was Thomas Mann Randolph Jr.

CHAPTER ONE
Give me Liberty or Give me Death

Governor Patrick Henry was such an important person in the founding of our Country's history I am respectfully including his address to the Virginia Ratifying Convention's first President of the American Congress, Peyton Randolph. This address was given on March 23, 1775 in Williamsburg Virginia.

Congressional President Payton Randolph at this time was considered by many to be the first President of America. This address was from the recollections of President Thomas Jefferson. This speech gave one of the best exponents of the reasons and the compassion that gave birth to the Revolutionary War.

Governor Patrick Henry's address goes as follows:

"Mr. President: No man thinks more highly than I do of the patriotism, as well as abilities, of the very worthy gentlemen who have just addressed the House. But different men often see the same subject in different lights; and, therefore, I hope it will not be thought disrespectful to those gentlemen if, entertaining as I do, opinions of a character very opposite to theirs, I shall speak forth my sentiments freely, and without reserve. This is no time for ceremony. The question before the House is one of awful moment to this country. For my own part, I consider it as nothing less than a question of freedom or slavery; and in proportion to the magnitude of the subject ought to be the freedom of the debate.

It is only in this way that we can hope to arrive at truth, and fulfil the great responsibility which we hold to God and our country.

Should I keep back my opinions at such a time, through fear of giving offence, I should consider myself as guilty of treason towards my country and of an act of disloyalty toward the majesty of heaven, which I revere above all earthly kings.

Mr. President, it is natural to man to indulge in the illusions of hope. We are apt to shut our eyes against a painful truth, and listen to the song of that siren till she transforms us into beasts. Is this the part of wise men, engaged in a great and arduous struggle for liberty?

Are we disposed to be of the number of those who, having eyes, see not, and, having ears, hear not, the things which so nearly concern their temporal salvation?

For my part, whatever anguish of spirit it may cost, I am willing to know the whole truth; to know the worst, and to provide for it.

I have but one lamp by which my feet are guided; and that is the lamp of experience. I know of no way of judging of the future but by the past. And judging by the past, I wish to know what there has been in the conduct of the British ministry for the last ten years, to justify those hopes with which gentlemen have been pleased to solace themselves, and the House? Is it that insidious smile with which our petition has been lately received? Trust it not, sir; it will prove a snare to your feet. Suffer not yourselves to be betrayed with a kiss.

Ask yourselves how this gracious reception of our petition comports with these war-like preparations which cover our waters and darken our land. Are fleets and armies necessary to a work of love and reconciliation? Have we shown ourselves so unwilling to be reconciled, that force must be called in to win back our love? Let us not deceive ourselves, sir.

These are the implements of war and subjugation; the last arguments to which kings resort.

I ask, gentlemen, sir, what means this martial array, if its purpose be not to force us to submission? Can gentlemen assign any other possible motive for it? Has Great Britain any enemy, in this quarter of the world, to call for all this accumulation of navies and armies? No, sir, she has none. They are meant for us; they can be meant for no other.

They are sent over to bind and rivet upon us those chains which the British ministries have been so long forging. And what have we to oppose to them? Shall we try argument? Sir, we have been trying that for the last ten years. Have we anything new to offer upon the subject? Nothing. We have held the subject up in every light of which it is capable; but it has been all in vain. Shall we resort to entreaty and humble supplication?

What terms shall we find which have not been already exhausted?

Let us not, I beseech you, sir, deceive ourselves. Sir, we have done everything that could be done, to avert the storm which is now coming on.

We have petitioned; we have remonstrated; we have supplicated; we have prostrated ourselves before the throne, and have implored its interposition to arrest the tyrannical hands of the ministry and Parliament.

Our petitions have been slighted; our remonstrance's have produced additional violence and insult; our supplications have been disregarded; and we have been spurned, with contempt, from the foot of the throne. In vain, after these things, may we indulge the fond hope of peace and reconciliation? There is no longer any room for hope. If we wish to be free if we mean to preserve inviolate those inestimable privileges for which we have been so long contending if we mean not basely to abandon the noble struggle in which we have been so long engaged, and which we have pledged ourselves never to abandon until the glorious object of our contest shall be obtained, we must fight! I repeat it, sir, we must fight!

An appeal to arms and to the God of Hosts is all that is left us! They tell us, sir that we are weak; unable to cope with so formidable an adversary. But when shall we be stronger? Will it be the next week, or the next year? Will it be when we are totally disarmed, and when a British guard shall be stationed in every house? Shall we gather strength by irresolution and inaction?

Shall we acquire the means of effectual resistance, by lying supinely on our backs, and hugging the delusive phantom of hope, until our enemies shall have bound us hand and foot? Sir, we are not weak if we make a proper use of those means which the God of nature hath placed in our power.

Three millions of people, armed in the holy cause of liberty, and in such a country as that which we possess, are invincible by any force which our enemy can send against us. Besides, sir, we shall not fight our battles alone. There is a just God who presides over the destinies of nations; and who will raise up friends to fight our battles for us.

The battle, sir, is not to the strong alone; it is to the vigilant, the active, the brave. Besides, sir, we have no election. If we were base enough to desire it, it is now too late to retire from the contest. There is no retreat but in submission and slavery! Our chains are forged! Their clanking may be heard on the plains of Boston! The war is inevitable and let it come! I repeat it, sir, let it come.

It is in vain, sir, to extenuate the matter. Gentlemen may cry, Peace, Peace but there is no peace. The war is actually begun! The next gale that sweeps from the north will bring to our ears the clash of resounding arms! Our brethren are already in the field!

Why stand we here idle? What is it that gentlemen wish? What would they have? Is life so dear, or peace so sweet, as to be purchased at the price of chains and slavery?

Forbid it, Almighty God! I know not what course others may take; but as for me, give me liberty or give me death!"

CHAPTER TWO
PREDICAMENT A HOUSE DIVIDED

In the year 1861, few in the Appalachian community wanted to go to war with the North. Again, most were just protecting their land and families. They were not out for blood! It was a series of most unfortunate decisions and events by others that forced most families to have to make life changing choices to defend their homes, as well as preserve the rights, and liberties of free people.

They did not own slaves and did not know anyone who did. Most of them were farmers when the hell hounds of war came to harass them.

There were members in the same families of differing persuasions. Some members wanted to join the Confederate South and other members wanted to join the Northern Union.

Some family members just wanted to be neutral or left alone and not join either side. One neighbor of the Confederate persuasion, Captain Ezekiel "Zeke" Counts, was one of the more out spoken opponents of the Northern aggression.

Zeke was born February 3rd 1828 in Russell County, Virginia. He was a farmer and served several terms as a constable. He organized a company of Confederate soldiers at Sandlick, Virginia. This was in June of 1862, not long after the war started.

Zeke Counts was promoted to full Captain on April 1, 1863. A nephew of his described Zeke as "brainy and resolute but nearly too quick tempered".

Zeke's son, John, eager for the approval of his father, joined his father's unit. There he served as a messenger or dispatch bearer and was a caretaker of the horses.

The Virginia State Line was abolished on February 28, 1863; Captain Zeke Count's company was reorganized into Company E, Virginia's 21st Cavalry Regiment under Colonel William E. Peters.

They fought in Logan and McDowell counties of West Virginia, Southwest Virginia, and Eastern Tennessee.

Captain Zeke Counts became known by the Union side and locals as "Devil Zeke" because of his guerrilla tactic type of warfare. They would lie in wait in the familiarity of the natural woods and fire upon the enemy. The element of surprise unnerved the enemy and always caught them off guard. Then, they would melt back into their natural habitat and foliage of the mountains. Being very familiar with the terrain due to hunting there for years, they had become masters at camouflage.

This group of men continuously scouted the country side and exchanged gunfire with any Unionists that they encountered encroaching upon their land.

After about a year in the 21st Virginia Cavalry, Captain Counts was reported to have deserted.

He left the 21st Virginia Cavalry, but his company remained intact and continued operating as guerillas in Buchanan, Russell, and Wise Virginia counties. He had known these areas like the back of his hand.

On April 14, 1864, Confederate Colonel Edmundson reported to the Secretary of War that Captain Counts was absent without leave and within the enemy's lines. The Colonel further requested the Captain's name be dropped from the rolls of the Confederate Armed Services.

As it turned out, Captain Counts actually had left the 21st Virginia Cavalry; but he and a small group of his company remained intact.

Following this, they had proceeded to operate as guerrillas in Buchanan, Russell, and Wise Virginia counties, all his well-known "old stomping grounds".

This battalion continued operating in Buchanan, Russell, and Wise Counties also occasionally scouted areas into McDowell, Logan and Tazewell counties.

As a note of interest, 1st Lt. William Anderson "Devil Anse" Hatfield of the famed Hatfield and McCoy feud left his command of the Company B 45th Battalion Virginia Infantry to form a home guard unit that cooperated with Captain Count's guerrillas.

During one of these operations, Captain Counts and his men arrested my 3rd Great Grandfather James Wheeler Hale and his brother Isaac Muncy Hale. Captain Counts demanded Isaac Muncy and James Wheeler Hale join the Confederates.

They refused to join him and the confederates, so Captain Counts had them sent to prison. They were held in a make shift cell in a railroad car for three days with little food or water. After three days, they relented and joined Captain Count's group. They joined with a secret plan to escape at the first opportunity.

Just a few days later during the night, they attempted to escape but were caught by the night guards. This time they were placed on a train and transported to a prison.

They were very fortunate to escape with their lives as it was told that Captain Counts would personally insist on having deserters shot on the spot.

Sometime during this train ride to the prison, both James Wheeler and Isaac Muncy Hale escaped by jumping from the moving train. Because they were both now considered deserters, James Wheeler and his brother Isaac Muncy Hale had no choice but to immediately leave home or face death by execution.

They left for Kentucky in the dark of night by the light of the moon. On June 1, 1862, they both joined the 39th Company Kentucky Infantry Union Army.

For almost a year in the summer of 1863, Margaret Hale, my 3rd great grandmother was home alone with all of her children. Like other women during the war, Margaret had been elected by a unanimous family decision "head of household pro tempore" to carry the burden of all the chores on the farm and in the home.

Not long after her husband left for Kentucky, Margaret was attacked by a group of Confederate soldiers. They were searching for her husband and his brother. They damaged everything and forcibly took all of her food and goods. They then threatened to burn down the house with her and her family inside it.

As soon as the soldiers left, the family greatly feared the soldiers would return to carry out their threats.

Because of this grave threat, Margaret and her loved ones immediately began to pack their belongings.

Packing only the most necessary items, Margaret, her children, both of her parents, and Uncle William Hale saddled up their horses and quickly traveled through Pound Gap into Letcher County, Kentucky.

CHAPTER THREE
THE MASSACRE AT DEADMAN'S HOLLOW

For several months, Margaret's cousins John and Andrew (Andy) Blair were hiding in the mountains in an attempt to stay out of the war. They basically just wanted the war to pass them by. John and Andy's parents were Jacob Blair and Jane (McClanahan) Blair. John Blair was a deserter from the Company, 34th Virginia E. He was married to Sarah Gilbert and had at least one child. It is believed that Andrew was not married.

Along with the Blair brothers were Harrison Bowman, his brother John and one Englishman Yankee deserter whose name is unknown at the time of this writing. These five men were on the run from both sides - the Union and the Confederacy!

They had been on the run apparently for several months. It was the last of winter with spring due to arrive within the next month or so. They had been so cautious with their chosen hiding places.

How much longer would this ungodly business of war continue? People were dying and people were killing other people. Brother against brother and neighbor against neighbor. When would all this madness cease?

There are many fearful things in life but having to hide in the cold and darkness constantly listening to every branch that snapped and movement in the dead leaves both above and below you had to be the scariest part. Constantly living in fight or flight is no way to live at all.

It was an unending, constant barrage of sounds. Sounds they were accustomed to hearing day in and day out but the constant terror that the next time it may not be a squirrel or a deer or a bear -- it may be the bullet of an assassin who has come to extrapolate what they think is justice. Justice punishable by death just because they didn't want to take someone else's life for someone else's so called "cause".

Without leaves and foliage to hide under it had to be getting harder and harder to keep the panic down from being discovered, checking every potential hiding spot. On March 1st 1864, they built up a small camp under a cliff of shelving rock deep in the heavily timbered woods near Alleys Creek in Deadman's Hollow, Virginia. Deadman's Hollow is just east of Cranes Nest.

They carefully, while quietly, worked quickly to camouflage the entrance to their new hiding place. Limbs, tree stumps, rocks, and bark skins from trees worked wonders to hide the men and shield them from hunters for their souls. Oh the evil that lurks in the hearts and minds of some people.

It had to be their earnest hope that the war would end soon and peace would come to the land. They wanted to return to their wives, children and families. With spring returning it would be much easier to conceal their presence in the forest. If they could just hold out just a little bit longer...........

Not long after they finished the camp, a local hunter (a man believed to be named Lark Adkins) came upon their camp while he was hunting game.

He recognized the Bowman and Blair brothers. The hunter gave his word to the men that he would not tell anyone of their hideout.

Unfortunately, this hunter was a Confederate supporter. As soon as he arrived back home from his hunting trip, he revealed the hiding place of the Blair and Bowman brothers along with the Yankee at Deadman's Hollow. He also informed a group of Confederate sympathizers of their location. This same group just happened to be some of the men with Captain Zeke Counts outfit.

Folks in the community had also been complaining of the thefts of food items from their barns and storage cellars. They complained the items were missing mostly during the night time. This charge was claimed against the deserters.

Whether it was true or not that the deserters were responsible for the thefts are left to conjecture.

The next day Captain Counts group of armed men caught Samuel Bowman (a relative of the Bowman brothers) tending the Mill owned by my 4th Great Grandfather, Rueben H. Powers. They questioned him about the whereabouts of the Blair and Bowman brothers.

Samuel denied knowing their location. He refused to tell the party of Confederate sympathizers any information. Thus, he was first hung with a belt around his neck until he was almost unconscious. They then tortured and interrogated him for several hours. He still would not give up the location of his relatives, that is, if he even knew their location.

The men were on the move frequently changing places and it is quite possible that Samuel did not know where the men were hiding out.

They let Samuel recover somewhat and then told him to leave. Beaten, cut, and near death Samuel started to leave, walking toward his home Samuel must have feared that at any moment he would be shot in the back, once he got near his home he fell to the ground lifted his hands up to pray. They shot and killed him while he was on his knees in prayer.

Later, the same group of Confederate sympathizers crept stealthily through the night and located the camp back in the rugged mountain. This is where they then patiently waited for the break of day to start their attack.

After scouting the camp and verifying that all five men were present, the group surrounded the camp with nothing but the vilest of intentions. They were not taking any prisoners..........dead or alive.

I often ask myself what drives men to do the horrible things they do.

No stories of what that last night was like for both parties exist but one would assume that the anxiety and tension must have been extremely high.

Did the Blair and Bowmen brothers really believe the hunter would not give away their secret location? Did they argue about staying or leaving? One thing is for sure; their minds had to be racing over and over again the encounter with the hunter.

Did the confederate sympathizers second guess their humanity knowing that in the morning they would be shooting these five men like "fish in a barrel"? The answer to that question we will never know; but we do know how the next day played out. It would have been very cold that morning at over 1,600 feet above sea level and more than likely fog and fresh snow along with the dew covered the ground.

At the break of day, Harrison Bowman was first to come out from under the cave, he had just stoked the fire and put on a pot of coffee. As he stepped up on a log and stretched, the first shot rang out hitting its target and Harrison fell directly to the ground. Immediately, after hearing this shot, both of the Blair brothers got up and took off running. The sympathizers stormed the camp from all directions.

Somehow the Blair brothers ran through a gap between several of the sympathizers as they charged the camp. Once at the camp they shot Harrison again, killing him. John Bowman was the next one to be shot and killed.

After they had shot the Yankee, he fell and begged for time to pray. They agreed to his request and after a few minutes they killed him.

The Blair brothers ran around the bend and actually had nearly gotten out of sight. They came to a stop and lay still on the ground except for breathing heavily they would not have made a sound in their attempt to hide.

I feel sure they could feel their hearts pounding inside their chests and the blood coursing through their veins as raw fear and terror gripped them in response to the reality of their situation. Their friends lie dead or almost dead. Maybe they were just wounded. Afraid to call out to them they lie quietly, confused as to whether they should chance it and run or not, afraid the very sound of their hearts or their very breath would betray them unto death.

They were sweating which made the cold chill of the morning even more frigid. Their teeth probably began to chatter. Keeping their eyes focused in the direction from which they just came from they would have whispered to each other about what to do next..........when the killers called out to them.

Their voices echoing through the empty forest called over and over again reassuring them of protection and kind treatment if they would simply give themselves up.

After some time of laying on the frigid, wet ground the Blair brothers accepted the proposed solemn promise of protection; they had no other choice, they gave up and walked back towards the killers.

Suddenly the forest seemed to come alive with the sounds of the wild life hidden there. Somewhere off in the distance you could hear the caw of the ravens and the screams of the captured prey from the claws of a hawk high up in the air.

A large tree limb broke and fell to the ground with a thud. The killers had caught their prey as well without even a fight.

The Blair brothers were weak from being on the run for months and didn't have the strength to run much further in an attempt a get away! Or were they in agreement about their safety from the promise that no harm would come to them if they gave up? Did they make the correct decision?

No, the killers had no intention of honoring their promise of protection and kind treatment. Just moments after they arrived back at the camp, the brothers were unmercifully beaten and executed.

Once the killers returned home, they reported their actions to their command, community and their family members.

Later, several men from the community headed out to Deadman's Hollow. They buried the dead men there, except for Harrison Bowman; he was taken to and buried at Old Henry Adkins Place.

CHAPTER FOUR
CRANES NEST BATTLE

The November 8th 1864 Cranes Nest Battle was between Union Captain Alf Killen and some Confederates under the command of a man named Major Clarence Prentice. The Confederates had somewhere between one hundred and two hundred soldiers; Captain Killen had around fifty men. They were greatly outnumbered but it was their homes, families, and way of life they had to protect. Most of these men lived in the area and were simply protecting their own homes and farms.

On the eve of November 7th 1864, both parties were camped near each other; the Confederates received word that Captain Killen and his men would be coming in the morning at dawn.

The Confederates set a trap in the dead of night, flanking on both sides of the wood lines, waiting in the woods for Captain Killen and his men to pass by them. They also had several men posing as decoys standing around a camp fire at the end of the road. Then, early in the dawn of the morning while the dew was still fresh on the ground, the Union men started to pass by the Confederates who were waiting to bushwhack them. Several of the Union men opened fire on the men standing around the camp fire killing one man and wounding another. The Confederates then opened fire on them raining down bullets from all directions.

It has been reported that nine of Captain Killen's men were killed, and many were wounded. Some escaped by running to the Cranes Nest River and attempting to swim away.

Most of the men that managed to get away down the Cranes Nest River departed the area and did not return after the war.

CHAPTER FIVE
BAD BLOOD COMES HOME

Several years before their killing, John and Andrew's brother Isaac Blair enlisted with Company A of Virginia's 51st Infantry Regiment on July 16th 1861 but mustered out only two weeks later. Isaac Blair was in Captain Zeke Counts' Company for a short time. Isaac Blair and Captain Counts apparently had a personality conflict or to put it mildly, "a difference of opinion," and Isaac then deserted. Isaac Blair was married to Martha Smith; they had at least one son.

Their brother George Washington Blair enlisted in 1862 with the Company A of Virginia's 34th Regiment Cavalry. He stayed with this outfit until the end of the war.

Captain Counts was always on the lookout for deserters including Isaac Blair. On one occasion, in an attempt to arrest Isaac Blair, a confederate named David Smith shot and seriously wounded him. Somehow Isaac managed to escape from David Smith's attempt on his life. He recovered from his wound and remained in hiding; which was probably the best decision he had made in quite a long time.

Shortly after the war ended in 1865, as it would turn out, Zeke Counts and Isaac Blair had an encounter at Old John Smith's Place. No one knows for sure if they were both looking for each other or if Isaac was still trying to stay out of Zeke's way. Was it just some sick joke played by destiny herself?

Isaac had suspicions that Zeke ordered the killing of his brothers John and Andrew just two years earlier at Deadman's Hollow. In addition, he was well aware that Zeke had been looking for him during the last year of the war.

With the South being on the losing side of the war, Zeke was obviously still holding a grudge against Isaac for deserting. Their paths crossed at Old John Smith's place. Old John Smith's place was owned by Isaac's father-in-law and I believe Zeke would have known this fact. They had words, and a serious altercation began leading to an old fashioned fist fight. The fist fight took a deadly turn for the worst with Zeke stabbing Isaac Blair to death.

Shortly after the killing of Isaac Blair, Zeke moved his family out west to Kansas and changed his name to Zeke Kountz.

Many believe this was done to avoid any retribution from the remaining Blair family, mainly Jacob Blair.

One story is told that Jacob Blair another brother to Isaac, John, and Andrew came after Zeke, looking to kill him. Unlike his brothers Jacob Blair was a fighting man.

Jacob served four years during the war and was in many of the large battles. One of his duties was as a lead tracker or scout. They say he could track a man through the summer woods as well as tracking a man through snow.

Margaret's sister Phoebe Yates married Alexander Johnson Skeen. He fought for the South with the Company A of Virginia's 51st Infantry Regiment.

Margaret's sister Nancy Yates married William Harrison Belcher. He fought for the South in Company B of Virginia's 36th Infantry Regiment.

Margaret's brother Andrew Jackson Yates fought for the North with the 39th Kentucky Infantry.

James Wheeler Hale returned from the War to Margaret's temporary home in Kentucky in 1865. They then returned to their Virginia home in the spring of 1866.

CHAPTER SIX
MARGARET'S STORY

At nearly ninety years of age Margaret starts her June 16th 1925 story as follows:

"According to what I heard my grandmother Nancy Sutherland Yates say, the Sutherlands and Yates came to Virginia from North Carolina – I do not know what county. My father John Yates was born April 13, 1800. My mother, Margaret Blair Yates, was born in Russell County, Virginia, March 13, 1811. My grandmother Nancy Sutherland Yates died in September of 1861, at Elias Green's on Caney Creek. She claimed to be 96 years old. My child Ellen was a baby then, and it was the first year of the War.

As long as I remembered knowing her, she had a cough, and it was most probably consumption (old timer's term for Tuberculosis or TB) that killed her.

She belonged to the Dumps Creek Baptist church. She was a small woman but very active.

Father lived on Dumps Creek near Carbo, Virginia until he moved to Hatchet Branch on McClure. My sister Phoebe was a baby at that move, and I was the first of the children born at Hatchet, in a log house. Daddy bought the land there from Nat Hammond and his wife Hannah Hammond. They were then living near the present graveyard at Nora, Isaiah Hammond then lived there too. Later the Hammonds moved to Missouri. I was big enough to know them when they left.

They were among the first settlers on McClure. Esau Hammond lived awhile at George W. Smith's on Smith Ridge. He sold out to Uncle George W. Smith and went to Missouri just after the other Hammonds moved there.

John Hammond moved to Stratton a little later: then sold out and went to Greenbrier, West Virginia.

His wife was named Peggy. Uncle Cage Ervin was living at Stratton when I can first remember. After five or six years, he went back to Russell or the head of the mouth of Caney.

Aunt Betsey Sutherland stayed with us a long time; then moved down to Nora and stayed with Grandma Yates.

Just the two of them stayed there together for several years. Jennie Ervin stayed with them some. Aunt Betsey Sutherland came and stayed one winter with Pa. She was very industrious, carding and spinning much wool. She was very kind to us children and I thought as much of her as I did my mother.

She was a common sized woman. She coughed up blood before she died. I was about six years old at her death.

She had one daughter, Jane or Jennie. She married Wash Neece, son of Henry Neece, and brother of Henry Neece, who married Nancy Ervin.

Old Henry Neece lived on ridge at head of Blair's Branch and sold his farm to Lihu Long, and I think Henry Neece went to Missouri with some other Longs. Wash Neece had two children at least, but I don't know their names. He moved to Johnson County, Kentucky during the Civil War and never came back to Virginia.

Billy Vanover came and settled at Roaring Fork at Uncle Cage's place. Jess Kelley lived on Roaring Fork about the same time. After Jess left, Billy Counts moved in before I was married. Johnson Skeen moved to Hatchet when Daddy left. Daddy had a lot of trouble trying to get title to his land there. He had 3200 acres run out and made a trade with Dale Carter, who claimed title to it, to give him $100.00 in cash for it.

Daddy got busy and sold ten of his steers to get the $100.00 and when Dale Carter came back again, he handed Dale the money.

Dale took the money, stuck it in his pocket and said, "John, I've got the money now- get the title the best way you can." Daddy jerked off his hunting shirt and said. "I'll have my title, or my money back, or blood one." I never saw him so mad. It scared us children pretty bad. Dale handed his money back and left, and Pa never could get any title. He got tired of waiting for a title and just left and came out on Caney Ridge.

Grandpa Blair lived at Nora, it was called the Ziah Hammond Place. It was up on a bank above the Sulphur spring. He had lived previously on Clinch River in Russell County.

He came to Virginia from North Carolina. His wife's name was Margaret or Peggy Walker, children's names unknown. In 1862, Grandpa Jacob Blair died at the age of about 82 at Betsy Chaney's on Blair Ridge, where Jasper Sutherland first settled.

He was buried there. Grandma Peggy Blair died after the war-about 1868-at the age of about 104 at Daddy's on Caney Ridge and was buried at Puther Place.

Daddy sold his land at Nora-about 700 acres-to my husband for $400.00. He bought this land from Nat and Zaih Hammond before they left for Missouri.

Aunt Adeline McClanahan, one of Daddy's cousins, lived at the Dave Smith place.

Her husband Ben McClanahan accidently shot himself with a muzzle-loading rifle. Daddy went to Lebanon for Dr. Kernan, but Uncle Ben died in a day or two. He was a blacksmith. I was about twelve years old then.

Aunt Adeline stayed there several years and then sold her land to Uncle George Smith and went back to Russell County. She had at least two children, George and Jim.

They sympathized with the Yankees in the Civil War and had to go to Kentucky and never came back.

The first settlers on McClure farmed a little, but mostly hunted. They cleared the little level bottoms along the creeks and branches. Most of the hunters came from the Clinch River settlements.

Among them were: Eph Kiser, Noah Kiser, Dan Kiser, Warren Kiser, Jim Sutherland, Bill Sutherland, Lige Sutherland and Uncle Dan Sutherland. Uncle Dan was Daddy's uncle and we were always glad to see him come. He was a small man and rather talky.

He didn't hunt much, but he liked bear-meat and venison very much and usually when he would come, he would bring a poke of apples, which were a rarity on McClure and for which he always wanted a mess of venison.

One day Warren Kiser was hunting a buck, but found a rattlesnake which bit him. Daddy and other hunters with him hurried him back to the house and gave him some brandy and camphor. He got scared and sent for his people who lived on Clinch River. When they arrived he was better, though his foot was badly swelled. He was sitting with his foot propped up in a chair and singing at the top of his voice when they came, which assured his folks that he was not bad off, and he went home horseback next day.

Daddy was a great hunter. He spent most of his time hunting. There were plenty of bears, deer, panthers, turkeys, and other varmints in the woods.

When I was about six or seven years old he killed a buffalo at the Three Forks of Buffalo Creek-that is how the creek got its name. It had a big track.

Daddy belonged to the McClure Baptist Church. He was baptized by Alex Vance at the mouth of Hatchet at the same time he baptized Sallie Green, Betsy Rose, Pop Hicks, and Vina Hicks, the last two being daughters of Clabe Hicks. My mother joined the Dumps Creek Baptist Church before moving to McClure. My father never held, nor asked for, any office. He delighted too much in his main occupation, hunting, to take time for public life.

In my youth, there was but little store clothing in our neighborhood. The men tanned leather and made their own and their family's shoes.

Each family raised its own flax and made its own tow-shirts and linen clothing. Sheep were raised from which the wool was sheared and carded into rolls, then spun into thread, then woven or knit into clothing.

The nearest store was at Lebanon, about twenty-five miles away and only connected with our neighborhood with a bridle-path.

We would take sang, bees-wax and hides to Lebanon and bring back salt, coffee, baled-cotton, dye-stuff and other store things. The settler who planted an orchard was always rewarded with a crop of fruit. Apples and peaches never failed. The woods were full of mast in the fall and winter.

It never failed until the war came up. There were very few parties in my day and time. We young folks worked hard all day and we felt good in going to bed at night. On Saturdays and Sundays, if there was a meeting in ten miles, we went to it, and then back home.

Some of the old songs we sung at such meetings were: The old Ship of Zion, Amazing Grace, and The old Church Yard.

Sometimes some of the neighbors would have chopping's, log rolling's and quilting's at which all the other neighbors would help. When a couple was married, all the neighbors were invited to the bride's home, where the marriage ceremony was performed. A fine dinner was always prepared. Then the next day the crowd would go to the groom's home where another fine dinner was set.

There was rarely ever a party, or dance, during a wedding celebration. I was never at a party in my young days. My sister Phoebe and brother Jonathan went to a few.

No drunkenness was seen those days. There was plenty of liquor and brandy, but no one used to an excess. Uncle Cage Ervin sometimes got too full.

Sim Dyer got too drunk one time at a log-rolling at Rainwater Ramsey's on Nealy Ridge and threw a plow over his head and killed Bill Sutherland's horse.

Most of the people in my neighborhood did not want to go into the army during the Civil War. Zeke Counts stirred up the people and tried to get them to enlist in the Rebel Army.

He was called by some of the people "Devil Zeke". He was made captain and helped to force several of the men into the army. At one time, his company was in Wyoming County, West Virginia, and my husband Jim Hale and his brother Isaac Hale had been out there visiting relatives and on their trip back home met Zeke Count's company. He tried to get them to join his company and when they refused, he arrested them and put them in a rail pen for three days, feeding them only parched corn. In order to get out, they agreed to join his company, but they did not stay with it long.

My uncle Isaac Blair was a member of his company for a while, but had trouble with him and quit.

Just after the war closed, they met at Old John Smith's place in Russell County and had a fight in which Devil Zeke killed Uncle Isaac.

Two other uncles of mine, John and Andy Blair, near the end of the war joined a band of men who were lying out to keep out of the war. There were five in this band, those besides my two uncles being: Harrison Bowman and his brother, and a bounty jumper, or Yankee deserter, whose name I do not remember. They were camping out in the woods on alleys Creek of Cranes Nest. One day a sheep-hunter discovered their hiding place, but promised not to tell on them. The next day a crowd came and killed them all, and they were buried there.

Jim Smith had started with the Rebels, but before he got there he fell down and accidentally shot himself in the neck.

Berry Vance helped him pick out the shot. Others in this crowd were: Jack Frye, Si Boggs, John McFall, and Lark Adkins. At this time I was in Johnson County, Kentucky.

My husband James Hale left our home on Ramsey Ridge on June 1, 1862 and went to Louisa, Kentucky where he joined Captain Nathaniel Collin's company of Union men. Isaac Hale, Dave Taylor, James W. Hale, and Andy Yates, my brother, went with him and all joined the Yankees.

James Hale was in the army three years, but was never in a battle. Andy Yates was in the army three years also, and was in two or three skirmishes. I left home in the summer of 1863.

Jack Frye, John McFall and other Rebel sympathizers came in my house on Ramsey ridge and tore up everything, and took all my meat, meal, dried apples and other food-stuff.

They threatened to burn the house right then, but John McFall said: "Don't bother her, boys; let her go to the damned Yankee army." As soon as I could get ready I left. Those in my neighborhood going with me were: Daddy and Mother and their family, William G. Hale and his family.

We traveled on horseback through Pound Gap into Letcher County, Kentucky. I never saw a wagon in my life until I went down there. We rented a farm of Billy Burchett near White House Shoal, and lived there three years.

After the war ended, my husband came to me, and we came back to Virginia in the spring of 1866. My brothers Lige and Zack came with us, but Daddy fattened his hogs and came back late in the spring.

We went to the mouth of Open Fork and stayed there purt nigh four years. Daddy went back to his old farm on Caney Ridge. When he came back, he found that someone had stolen twenty of his bee-stands.

My brother-in-law, Johnson Skeen, had looked after Daddy's property while he was in Kentucky. Some of the other people who went away from our neighborhood during the war period were: Bill Taylor, Charles Taylor, Dave Taylor, and John Taylor, all crossing the Ohio and none returning: all the Gilliam's, Ira, Bill, Mart, and old Uncle Johnny. Bill and Mart died during the war, and the others came back after the end of the war.

During the latter part of the war, the only big fight in the county took place on Cranes Nest near where Allen Powers now lives. The Rebels had about a hundred men there, among them being Jack Frye and John McFall.

The Yankees had forty-some odd under Captain Nathaniel Collins, among them being Draper Powers, Alex Powers, John Powers, Charley Hibbitts and brother Henry. In this fight, five Yankees were killed, three of them being Charley Hibbitts, John Powers and brother Henry.

This fight took place in the spring of 1863. All the killed were buried there on the spot in holes. At the end of twelve days Daddy went to see if he could find Henry's body, but they were all so badly cut and beaten that he could not identify Henry. So several of the old men and women in the community got together, wrapped the dead in blankets and buried them on the spot, using camp puncheons to frame coffins for them. Some of these old men who helped bury the dead were: Wills Adkins and Davy Vance.

The first school building on McClure was built by John Hammond or maybe Simmy Dyer, Sammy Rose, George Smith, John Yates and Ben McClannahan.

It was built at the mouth of Buffalo Creek and made of spilt logs raised just high enough to walk under, and then daubed with moss. The schools taught there were on the subscription plan at $3.00 per month for three months.

I went three days to the first school taught there. The teacher was from Russell County, but I forget his name. I went about a month to Ben Haley there later, but he was so ill and mean to the scholars that they drove him back to Kentucky. Uncle Arch Hale, who then lived near the present Fremont, came and taught the school out. I never went over two months to school, all told, in my life.

Uncle G. Hale taught one term of three months at Buffalo. That was the last school taught there while I lived there. Harve Ball tried to teach a school there but did no good.

I was married to James W. Hale on February 2, 1855. I lacked from February 2nd to March 10th being twenty years old when I married. My husband was born December 21, 1824, in Russell County, Virginia. His parents were William G. Hale and Anna (Wheeler) Hale, his mother being the daughter of James and Polly (Amburgey) Wheeler, who lived on Lick Creek near St. Paul, Virginia. My father-in law, Billie Hale, was a Baptist preacher and lived on Ramsey Ridge. He performed the marriage ceremony for us and six of my brothers and sisters.

After marriage, we moved to Ramsey Ridge and lived there nine years, then went to Letcher County, Kentucky and stayed there during the war.

Then came back and settled at the mouth of Open Fork, lived there four or five years, then went to the ridge above the Powers settlement on Cranes Nest, from there we went to Lick Fork where I lost everything I had by high waters. We left there in 1923. My husband died on Bold Camp seventeen years ago. I have since broken my arm. We had nine children and they were:

William Hale was born February 6, 185?, on Ramsey Ridge. He lives on a farm on Cranes Nest.

He married Lindy Malissa Mullins and their children are Sarah, Martha, Delphia, Bertha, Jack (crippled), Ida, Monroe and Addis.

Mary Hale was born September 28, 1858. She married Sylvester Kilgore, a son of Billy and Nancy Kilgore.

John Hale was born November 27, 18??, He was a farmer. He married Betty Stanley, a daughter of Bill and Annie Stanley. Their children were Henry, Nannie, Orpha, Edward and Ira. (2) Mary Salyers, a daughter of Hannah Salyers, and their children were Lula, Hetty and Artie. Ellen Hale was born May 19, 1861. She married Little Basil Mullins. Both are still living on a farm on Cranes Nest.

Their children were Lydia, Margaret, Patton, Louvina and maybe another one or two.

Phoebe Hale, married Henry Kilgore, a son of Billy and Nancy Kilgore. Both are dead. Their children were Louisa, and Walker. Walker Kilgore and Salyers were the only grandchildren I had in the World War.

Andrew Hale lived on a farm on Alleys Creek near Nasbie, Virginia. He married Nancy Vanover, a daughter of Bill and Nancy Vanover. They are both dead. Their children were Lydia, Sallie, Edith May, Nora, Ocea and maybe others.

Elbert Hale is now living on a farm on Alleys Creek near Nasbie, Virginia.

He married (1) Sarah Belle Mullins, a daughter of Little Riley Mullins. Their children were James Estel, Burley Taft, and Thomas Guy. He married (2) Rebecca Hollyfield, a daughter of Tom Hollyfield of Scott County, Virginia. Their children were, Nancy, Margaret, Joseph and Mary. I have over one hundred great-grandchildren."

The End of Margaret's Story!

CONCLUSION

Margaret states that John, Andrew, and Isaac Blair were her Uncles. In reality, they were actually her cousins and she could have misspoken this on account of her advanced age.

Also, in one part of Margaret's story, she talks about traveling on horseback through Pound Gap from Virginia into Letcher County, Kentucky. This trip took place in 1863 and she stated it was the first time in her life she had seen a wagon.

I find that statement ironic because on May 14, 1892, another of my family stories called "Killing Moonshine Mullins" took place in a wagon at Pound Gap called "The Pound Gap Massacre".

During the Civil War and as is typical of other wars, catastrophic destruction, unspeakable horror, and murder are thus usually considered justified.

With the loss of thousands of young men, husbands, fathers, brothers, sons, mules, horses, and homesteads, the women and children had to fight to start over again.

Over 620,000 Americans were killed during the Civil War. Lots of brave men, women, and even children died on both sides as well as those who fought to stay neutral. There was a side of those who did not feel like they had a stake in that fight but were forced to fight anyway.

Many Southern men did not agree with slavery but felt they needed to fight to protect their homes and families.

Many did not fight because as Christian men they did not believe in the taking of a life for any reason whether it was believed to be justified or not. These men stood for righteousness.

Still, some paid the ultimate price for their Christian beliefs and they lost their own lives in the process, once the war landed on their doorsteps.

Many Southern men fought for the North because they believed all men should be free. Yet, many of these men paid the price for joining the Union and returning home after the war.

Some were killed in arguments once they returned home. Some never returned home at all out of fear of retaliation!

This war was not simply cut and dry or black and white. Many Southerners were being told that the Northern Army was burning everything in its path all throughout the Southern territories. Some fought because they were being attacked.

Honestly, there must always be room for dignity for all 620,000 Americans killed during the Civil War.

Just simply stating that this group was right and that group was wrong would not serve justice. It also would not accurately portray the real history involved.

My family members since the beginning of this country have been on both sides of nearly every conflict.

They were Native American Indians and New Settlers from Jamestown. They were Revolutionary soldiers and British soldiers, the war of 1812, they were Northern troops and Southern soldiers, U.S. soldiers and German soldiers, and they fought in WWI, WWII, the Korean War, the Vietnam War, the Persian Gulf War, and the War on Terrorism.

Whatever the reasons, the fact remains that during the Civil War 620,000 Americans died settling conflicts between 1776 and 1865.

That number climbs exponentially when you consider the number of future generations of children that were not born to the 620,000 Americans who died.

These events happened all due to man's inability to solve intellectually, socially, and spiritually it's ills of the time period. It was an extremely high cost of life to all to learn to live together as the Gettysburg address and our Constitution so eloquently state, "All men are created equal."

We must never forget that there were many different scenarios and reasons families chose to fight or try to stay out of the fight. Nevertheless, a lot of good-intentioned people died in between.

Some were a part of the fray........ some got caught up in the fray......... some just came unraveled due to the fray!

The end of the War was not the end to the hardships in the Appalachian Mountains. It was the start of the "Carpetbaggers."

Immediately after the war, many northerners headed to the Appalachian Mountains in search of economic gain.

Many of these Carpetbaggers were opportunists looking to exploit and profit from the reconstruction. The term "Carpetbagger" refers to Northerners that came into a community with only a carpet bag of possessions.

These men took control over their new surroundings often against the will of the people in the community. They would purchase land "dirt cheap" from Southerners that were down and out because of their war circumstances. Some came to invest and assist with reconstruction, but many were corrupt opportunists.

Life has never been easy for the people of Appalachia. Consequently, this was just one more battle that landed upon their doorstep.

SOURCES

Interview notes by my 3rd GGM Margaret (Yates) Hale written June 16, 1925.

Ancestry.com family Records.

Notes by my 1st cousin 5x Mary Jane (Blair) Ball.

Newspaper article, Dickinson County (unknown) by Jasper Sutherland 1921.

Virginia Governor Patrick Henry, Speech on March 23, 1775.

The Name and Family of Kennedy and Powers, written by Wade F. Kennedy 1941.

ACKNOWLEDGMENTS

To my wife and Co-Author Doris Gail Barber Baldwin, whose love and giving support make all things possible. A true Proverbs 31: 10-31 wife. She is also one my Editors.

To my daughter Amanda Baldwin, many thanks for your long hours and hard work.

To my son Roy Dean Baldwin, many thanks for your long hours and hard work.

Contact email:
Thebaldwinstories@gmail.com

Check out my other stories and books at:

http://thebaldwinstories.wix.com/author-blog

The eBook Pocahontas to Benjamin Bolling, describes her life's story and Major Benjamin Bollins' DNA connection to Pocahontas at:

http://www.amazon.com/dp/B01BQTYE4Q/

The eBook Devil's Ground: Arco Station describes different and strange circumstances, events, and happenings that I witnessed first-hand at:

http://www.amazon.com/-/e/B017PE3W7Q

The eBook Lora's Stories, an eBook with memoirs of Lora's life growing up as an Appalachian child. One that will make you laugh, cry, and bring you joy all at the same time. A real look into a women's heart at:

http://www.amazon.com/dp/B01C69BXRG

The eBook Killing "Moonshine" Mullins And the Aftermath covers the Ira Mullins family massacre. They were early settlers to Letcher County, Kentucky, Wise County, Virginia, and parts of southern West Virginia. This story is one of the wildest stories ever told to me as well as one of my absolute favorites at:

http://www.amazon.com/dp/B01AGSESVW

Friend me on my Facebook page at:

https://www.facebook.com/The-Baldwin-Stories

Please remember to write a review on Amazon. Thanks.

Back Cover: Picture of James Wheeler Hale and Margaret (Yates) Hale.

9 781537 476124